Twenty-five

A MEMOIR OF CANCER
in
POETRY

Beth MacDonald

Copyright © 2023 Beth MacDonald

All rights reserved. No part of this book may be used or reproduced in any manner whatsoever without the written permission of the author, except by reviewers, who may quote brief passages within reviews. For permission contact <u>northinkbooks.com</u>

ISBN: 978-1-7374760-6-1

Cover Design: Romy Klessen

Angel Design: Maria Filosa

First Printing

In memory of my mother,
Gail Nordlie

Dedicated to my sister,
Mary Swanson

With love to my family,
Mike MacDonald
Nicholas MacDonald
Samantha MacDonald Solberg

With thanks to the friend
who kept me surrounded by angels,

Maria N. Filosa

Twenty-five years ago my family went through a difficult time. At forty-one, I was diagnosed with cancer. In the months that followed, both my sister and my mother received similar diagnoses. My sister and I survived. My mother, Gail Nordlie, died August 27, 1998. This is the story of that year in poetry.

CONTENTS

Life's Ups and Downs	**1**/7
Mickey Kicked My Butt	**2**/9
Eyes of the CAT	**3**/10
Parking Karma	**4**/11
Stop, Drop, and Roll	**5**/12
Jay's Prank	**6**/13
Miss Demeanor	**7**/14
Watching Mom	**8**/15
1998: News Comes in Threes	**9**/16
Nil	**10**/17
False Bravado in the Hospital	**11**/18
Between Two Daughters	**12**/19
The Only Way	**13**/20
The Last Sense to Leave	**14**/21
A Walk with Dad	**15**/22
The Harvest Carnival	**16**/23
Buoyed	**17**/24
Friendly Fire	**18**/25
Losing My Neighbor	**19**/26
Smelling Funny	**20**/27
In My Daughter's Hand	**21**/28
An X-ray with Joan Didion	**22**/29
Intolerable Treatment	**23**/30
Cake and Flowers	**24**/32
Broken Vows and New Signs	**25**/33

 **Life's Ups and Downs**

I said I'd be a chaperone
    A woman to add balance
        I'd never hiked a mountain path—
    Never hoisted a large pack
Upon my untried lily back

I was wary, that is true
    Yet, most said I could do it
        I had doubts I'd be of aid—
    But commitments I had made
So, on my back this duty stayed

Up the Bighorns we hiked
    Our bodies ever higher
        It was harder than I'd thought
            To climb a mountain spire

            I trudged along, looking down
        I ignored the mountainous vantage
    Strange fungus, flowers, and the path
Were all that I could manage

The night came when
I could hike no more
My tired body shutting down

Help ascended
    From below
        To save this hobbled chaperone
            Orders, IVs, ambulance
                A rescue made of vowels
            The doctors said that I'd survive
        Of x-rays there was no need
    It was a classic they all knew—
High altitude disease

Had they checked
They might have found
The mass within me growing
Perhaps it was best not diagnosed
What good would've come from knowing?

 ## Mickey Kicked My Butt

All my family—one, two, three—
walked up the path in front of me.
I could not keep up,
tried though I may,
I could not survive
a Disney day.
I thought, *perhaps
I'm just getting old*,
but, Mike, years my senior,
his steps were bold.
It made no sense
that I could see.
  I trudged ahead—
   they blew past me.

Maybe by then
I already knew
that something sinister
inside me grew.
Lingering thoughts of health amiss,
could this be our last Christmas?
Circumstance soon
made it clear,
I should see a doc posthaste
next year.
But, did I go?
  Well, it took awhile—
   I was loathe to lose my Disney smile.

 **Eyes of the CAT**

I waited in the crowded room,
feeling all alone.
An eternity, it seemed to me—
a funny word at such a time.

Called to the table, high and flat
by tired techs, late for lunch.
Their eyes said, "Here's another one,
a likely hypochondriac."

They did not help me to the slab.
"You look fit enough," they sighed.
"Lie on your back, look straight up,
listen for commands." *I'll try*

The CAT moved slowly back and forth;
its red eye only I could see.
Orders came: "Hold your breath. You may breathe."
Not coughing was left up to me.

Slices of my chest on film.
Time to sit, to stand, to leave.
But now the techs ran to my side.
Their guilty eyes screamed—horrified!

A change in tone, in care and glance.
Further diagnosis unneeded.
Lunch no longer on their minds,
my terrible fate to them now ceded.

 **Parking Karma**

I drive into the open spot,
so convenient to the door.
The sign looming above my hood
states who this space is for:

> *CANCER PATIENTS ONLY*

I put the car in *R* to leave,
then stop, and shift to *P*.
I turn the key with trembling hands.
This space is meant for me.

 ## Stop, Drop, and Roll

I raise my sleeves; from across the room
comes the harried nurse's retort,
"Stop right now, she has no veins.
Within her chest, she'll need a port."

It isn't true—I do have veins.
They just retract when filled with fear.
They drop, they roll, they simply hide,
when IV needles come too near.

It's a personal safety net,
to keep my blood internal.
But when I'm under a doctor's care
the staff finds it infernal.

So, I had a port installed—
an IV needle landing pad.
Now, nurses give their drugs with ease,
even though my veins are bad.

 ## Jay's Prank

He grabbed the scarf
From atop my head
A little boy —
      in a grown man's body

The shock and sorrow
He could not hide
Teenage pain —
      in a grown man's body

His remorse and shame
His words confessed
He did not know, it was in jest
Becoming the man —
      to match his body

 ## Miss Demeanor

Every now and then,
once a month at best,
I'd have to leave the clinic
with tubes taped to my chest.

I tend to follow every rule.
With seatbelt laws comply,
but with tubes taped to my chest,
on those days, well, I wouldn't try.

I'd always hoped that I'd be stopped
by a super vigilant traffic cop
asking me to tell him why
on seatbelts I did not rely.

I'd open up my shirt to show
tubes taped neatly in a row,
show him where the needle's stuck,
and tell him—
    I DON'T GIVE A FUCK!

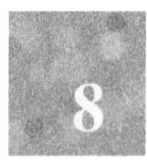 **Watching Mom**

She'd watched the children as they'd grown.
Of her grandkids she was proud.
She had often tucked them in at night
while Mike and I were theater-bound.

For years I'd watched her leave our house,
walk to hers, not far away—
her steps so strong, so quick, so sure.
But today I watched her graceless sway.

I watched her gait as she walked home
after taking care of me.
Sad I'm sick, she often says,
"Mary, too? How can this be?"

I watch her take our bitter cup,
drink it down—not make a fuss.
Given the choice, she'd be ill—
if she could give her life for us.

I watch the kitchen door swing wide,
the porch light darken, Mom go in.
I know she's safe within her home,
but fear she's not within her skin.

 **1998: News Comes in Threes**

In January I was told
Non-Hodgkins
Lymphoma
Fast-growing
    Treatable

In February my sister heard
The lump she felt was
Breast cancer
Malignant
    Beatable

In May our mother's tears revealed
What her words no longer could
Glioblastoma multiforme
Fast-growing, malignant
    Not treatable
    Not beatable

 **Nil**

I'd coughed for months,
but looked just fine.
I tired easily, but seemed well.
When the doctor said,
"Something's wrong,
your x-rays don't look right."
I thought her wrong.
How could it be?
What were the chances?

My sister visited
from the east.
She told us of a lump.
It was not her first—
she'd been fine before.
Besides, there was no way
we'd both be ill.
How could it be?
What were the chances?

Our mother sways—
her balance is off.
In her speech there's a slur.
A stroke, perhaps?
The scan says no.
Cancer, too, it seems,
deep within her brain.
How can it be?
What are her chances?

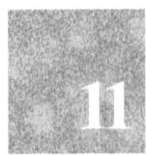 ## False Bravado in the Hospital

"We can do this,"
I said to my mother,
as she sat with shaved patches
her hair not covering.

"We can do this,"
I said to my mother,
as I stood with my head wrapped
my bald pate in hiding.

"We can do this,"
I said to my mother,
our eyes deep pools,
our tears not falling.

The doctor asks,
"What can you do?"
"We can live until we can't, sir.
That is all we can do."

 **Between Two Daughters**

My sister, needle pulled from port,
has only two days to recover
before walking down the jetway
to fly westward to our mother.

Mom waits in Dad's recliner now—
wishing, wanting, worried—
for the babe who kept her up at night,
the very first to whose side she'd scurried.

Guilty, Mom still wishes daily
that she could have been by Mary's side
when the surgeons cut her flesh away
leaving cancer one less place to hide.

Never wanting to make the choice,
yet forced by circumstance to choose—
to stay with me or to go to Mary—
knowing one would have to lose.

Ill herself, she worries still—she sits,
no longer can she pace the floor.
She wishes in silence for Mary to come;
wanting her eldest to walk through the door.

 **The Only Way**

Mom, I am sick,
but you won't see crying.

Mom, I am sick,
but you're the one dying.

The only way to let you go,
is to say, "I will not follow."

The only way to forgive myself,
is to say, "I did all I could."

Had I been well, your awful death
would have brought an end to me.

You gave your life, so that I might live.
I will not fail you by not trying.

The Last Sense to Leave

My sister and I sat
on the full-sized bed
our legs criss-crossed,
our now sparse hair
swathed in cotton turbans.

We may have had
tears in our eyes,
that detail now eludes,
but laughter is what I recall —
obnoxious, loud, and raucous.
Odd sounds in a hospice.

Mom died that morning
while we laughed
just one room away.
I know she heard us,
and was assured
by our joyous braying.

She allowed herself
to leave this realm,
struggled no more to stay alive.
The neighboring noise meant to her —
      her much-loved daughters would survive.

 ## A Walk with Dad

My father walks beside me
as we trail behind the casket.
The family follows,
we both know this,
but I cannot feel their presence.

I'm dressed in black, with chunky heels,
hair like a cat's—short and sleek.
My father's clad in his woolen suit—
pressed creaseless only four months ago,
by his wife, my mother.

I had been so close to Mom,
all of us—her kids—had been.
Our dad seemed but an afterthought,
the man who'd worked to pay the bills,
but often kept us all at bay.

Now his shoulder presses on mine
and I return that weight.
I lean on him as we stare ahead
toward the long, buffed-metal box
that holds the woman we both love.

I've not yet told my father
that my cancer has returned.
I'll let him lean upon my arm,
as long as I am able.
It's a lifetime guarantee—
        his or mine—time will tell.

 **The Harvest Carnival**

The tube is stitched
into my neck,
my blood seeps
all around it.

Black cherry Kool-Aid it flows
in straw-like tubes—
to-and-fro, a centrifuge,
a modern Tilt-a-Whirl.

Goldilocks stitches to end the day:
too few—blood oozes
too many—tissue dies
just right—I sleep the night away.
    Just right, just right, just right, I pray.

The surgeon's done, with force and might.
The tube's secured, the stitches tight—
a night in hell
with sterile sheets.
    The nurse tells me it's finally right.
        Good night, I say—
           good night, good night.

 **Buoyed**

isolated
yet not alone
Maria saw to that
    designing angels surrounded me
    sending crafted gifts by snail-mail
    and heart-felt wishes by PC

in church
each Sunday
the congregants prayed
    they spoke my name, they asked for grace
    and when the time came for my hospital stay
    they petitioned God to bless that space

at home
my family
kept fires tended
    Mike paid the constant medical bills
    and to keep my mind at ease
    our kids controlled their teenaged wills

they carried me upon their shoulders
buoyed me up from deep distress
my friends, my church, my family
raised me above the cancerous mess

 **Friendly Fire**

People talk of cancer
as an enemy to battle,
a foe to defeat,
a war to be won.

As I lie on clean sheets,
food brought to me on trays
by those who smile and wish me well,
I'll always choose this kind of hell.

I never want to go to war,
to meet and kill my enemies.
I certainly don't wish to face
unpinned grenades hurled at me.

On scarred lands I'll never tread,
dirty, scared, and bleeding.
I'd rather lie here sick in bed
with nurses my cares meeting.

I speak to my oncologist,
sharing thoughts about my treatment.
I think he'll say, "Oh yes, you're right,
this is a better kind of fight."

That's not, however, what he says,
he whose treatments use stem cells.
He says, "Given a choice of war or cancer,
war would be my choice of hells."

 **Losing My Neighbor**

She's alone, from the west,
in the room next to mine.
I smell whiffs of creamed corn,
hear words, "You'll be fine."

She speaks to the doctor;
she can't bear the stay.
"Your cells are rebuilding
You must give them a day."

I hear her cry softly,
"What is the point?
I can't take any more—
let me out of this joint!"

The intercom sounds: Code Blue, don't delay.
They cover her face—she got her way.

 **Smelling Funny**

Crushed up Fritos in a cup
Day old veggie stew
The odors coming off of me
Aren't from a kitchen brew

I'm dreaming of recovery
As I lie in bed
Smells will someday come from food
Not from me, but instead

Some say it's creamed corn they smell
Some say chicken soup
I think of brighter days ahead
When I will smell of soap and Joop!

 **In My Daughter's Hand**

I kept the family calendar,
scribbled notes in tiny boxes.
A habit born from experience,
one every mother knows.

A teenaged son, his license new,
his schedule all his own.
Computer on, in his room,
his friends on telephone.

New-teen daughter—constant rides,
activity her companion.
She sings, she acts, with toes on point,
round and round, she dances.

For years I'd kept us all in line,
from Scouts to art-filled classes.
Penciled, noted, folders filed—
appointments rarely missed or canceled.

October comes—November follows.
The calendar grows still,
though not for long—handwriting proves
my little girl's grown up too soon.

Hers is the hand that inks the boxes.
Precise and round she keeps life planned.
Her rides now come from her brother;
both fill the voids left by their mother.

 ## An X-ray with Joan Didion

I lie on the hard table
Locked in place
Body draped with lead
I dream of days when this is done
I crave normality instead

A day when I have hair
A day when time's all mine
A day when Mom returns to see
All has worked out fine

When I'm well
I'll have Mom back
How could that not be?
I've lived my whole life next to her
She'd not abandon me

Then it hits, Mom is gone
Death took her, never blinking
A half year passed without my mom
This year of magical thinking

 **Intolerable Treatment**

Twentieth scan,
the cough begins.
I tell the Radiologist. She says,
"Never mind:
      You have tolerated them so far."

X-ray treatments over,
I am coughing even more.
I tell my old Oncologist. He says,
"It's expected from the protocol:
      You have tolerated it so well."

I see a general practice doc—
My coughing keeps me up at night.
Is there something you can do? He says,
"Syrup, pills, but mainly time:
      You have tolerated much, that's true."

The coughing worsens,
nothing helps—
I choke and gasp for air.
Headaches start, my chest gets sore.
Fearing broken ribs and bleeding lungs,
      I can tolerate no more.

I call a Pulmonologist,
and ask when I might see him.
"It will be six months or more," he says.
Nothing sooner? I reply,
I'll be dead by then.
      I cannot tolerate delay.

I'm finally in,
the exam begins. The doctor says,
"You look well—why are you here?"
I explain; the doc seems bored.
Then my coughing starts:

> It grips my body
> I cannot stop
> I cannot breathe
> I cannot talk
> I choke
> I gasp
> I sob

The doctor looks at me and cries,
"Why didn't you come sooner?"
I've never been believed, I say.
I've spoken of my cough for months
My words barely tolerated—
not by them, not by you, and now I am berated?

                      I will tolerate no more.

 **Cake and Flowers**

He was eighty-two when my mother died.
Dad knew little of household chores:
cleaning, cooking, shopping.
But, within a year he'd mastered most.

On August twenty-third of nineteen-ninety-nine,
he baked a candled birthday cake:
chocolate, two-layered, frosted.
A gift for me, his little girl.

Four days later he took a bouquet
purchased at the grocery store—
roses, leatherleaf, baby's breath—
to his wife's park-like grave.

It was a sad first-anniversary gift
for one no longer by his side.
But, both were living tributes
to his daughter and his bride.

 **Broken Vows and New Signs**

Diagnosed with cancer,
I made one single vow;
illness wouldn't change me.
    To cancer I'd not bow.

Born on the cusp of Virgo,
August twenty-three,
my new natal day's November second,
    the day my cells returned to me.

Scorpio's my new horoscope.
But when I check the paper,
Cancer is the sign I see—
    even Virgo's turned to vapor.

I broke a vow I should not have made,
doubting the power of the disease.
I mourn for Mom, I cry with Mary—
    for cancer changes when it comes in threes.

www.ingramcontent.com/pod-product-compliance
Lightning Source LLC
Chambersburg PA
CBHW021135080526
44587CB00012B/1295